Maestro Segovia

Maestro
Segovia

compiled and edited by

Graham Wade

 Robson Books

Eugenio d'Ors y Rovira, the great Spanish philosopher and writer, once said, 'The song of the piano is a discourse, the song of the harp is an elegy, but the song of the guitar is a song.'

First published in Great Britain in 1986 by Robson Books Ltd., Bolsover House, 5–6 Clipstone Street, London W1P 7EB

British Library Cataloguing in Publication Data

Wade, Graham, *1940*–
  Maestro Segovia : sayings, anecdotes and
  impressions.
  1. Segovia, Andrés   2. Guitarists—Spain—
  Biography
  I. Title
  787.6 1 0924   ML419.S4

  ISBN 0-86051-386-6

Typeset by Spire Print Services, Ltd, Salisbury
Printed in Great Britain by St Edmundsbury Press,
Bury St Edmunds, Suffolk

Contents

Introduction

Andrés Segovia was born in Linares, Jaén, in the region of Spain known as Andalusia, on 21 February, 1893. From his early childhood Segovia was deeply responsive to the sound of the guitar. But at that time the instrument was not considered to be worthy of serious musical study and there were no competent teachers in the province of Jaén, nor in Granada where he went to live at the age of ten. It was in Granada that he acquired his first guitar and began the long journey of self-tuition. Within a comparatively short time he had developed a prodigious mastery and with the help of friends discovered the existence of several fine compositions for the guitar which surpassed the regional flamenco styles of playing.

By 1909, at the age of sixteen, Segovia was ready to make his public debut as a recitalist and appeared at the Centro Artístico in Granada. Concerts in Córdoba and Seville followed, and three years after his first concert, Segovia moved to Madrid and made his debut in the Spanish capital at the Ateneo. At this time he was presented with his first concert guitar of quality by Manuel Ramírez.

There were many struggles in these early years. The available repertoire was very slim and most people regarded the guitar as not suitable for the concert hall. Yet, despite several setbacks, Segovia continued to play recitals throughout Spain, and eventually managed to arrange a tour of various South American countries. In 1924 he made a resoundingly successful debut in Paris, a recital attended by many of the most distinguished musicians of that period. From about 1920 onwards, Segovia not only enriched the range of the guitar repertoire by transcribing and performing works by great composers of the past, but also persuaded his contemporaries to write new pieces for the instrument. Composers such as Federico Moreno Torroba and Joaquín Turina of Spain, Manuel Ponce of Mexico, Mario Castelnuovo-Tedesco of Italy, Heitor Villa-Lobos of Brazil, and Alexandre Tansman of Poland, all wrote significant compositions for him during this crucial time of struggle to establish the guitar as a musical force to be reckoned with.

Armed with this new repertoire, Segovia's international esteem rapidly increased. In 1926 he performed in Russia and Britain, in 1927 in Scandinavia, in 1928 came his first tour of the USA, and in 1929 Segovia made his first visit to Japan. Since that time, the sound of Segovia's guitar has been heard in almost every country in the world.

Segovia was the first guitarist to achieve true commercial success in the field of recording. In the 1930s he made many 78 rpm recordings, and from 1949 onwards became a prolific artist on the new revolutionary long-playing records. Between 1949 and 1979 he recorded about forty albums.

Throughout the years he continued his task of taking the guitar to the world's musical public. In 1985, at the age of ninety-two, he toured the United States,

England, and Italy, giving nearly twenty concerts in all. He has been equally industrious as an editor of music, dozens of his arrangements, transcriptions and editions having been published, particularly in the Segovia Archives Series issued by Schott since the 1920s. Through his example he has inspired the younger generations in many countries to take up the guitar. Such players as Julian Bream and John Williams were inspired by his playing and his teaching, to undertake an international career, as were many others.

As one of the greatest instrumentalists of the twentieth century, Andrés Segovia has received many honours from the international community, and is certainly the most distinguished guitarist in the history of music. He has received a host of honorary doctorates from the major universities of the world and his numerous medals of distinction include the Grand Cross of Isabel la Católica, Spain's highest civilian honour. In 1981 Andrés Segovia was created Marquis of Salobreña by His Majesty King Juan Carlos I of Spain, thus becoming the first guitarist to be elevated to the aristocracy for his contribution to music.

Such a celebrated world citizen has been interviewed for radio and the press many hundreds of times. Segovia delights in anecdotes, humour, and appropriate musical pronouncements. Most of his talking, as the world knows, has been through the eloquence of his guitar in recital. Yet his elegant wit and Andalusian dignity, his constant equilibrium between musical seriousness and a subtle, almost mischievous, sense of humour, have indeed in themselves become widely renowned. Segovia himself is a master linguist, at home especially in English and French; the quotations presented here have usually been delivered in his own impeccable and poetic English. For many of the quotations several sources could equally well be named, but I have chosen from specific publications where possible, in order to preserve precise reference points.

I am particularly grateful to Maestro Segovia for giving so generously of his time and hospitality in Madrid and London. I must also express appreciation to Señor Alberto López Poveda of Linares for his help with a wide range of sources of reference. A full list of acknowledgements is to be found at the end of the book.

GRAHAM WADE

November 1985

Impressions and Tributes

Max Nordau, the writer and philosopher, who attended Segovia's debut in Madrid in 1913, wrote:

'I say, and I do not believe I blaspheme in doing so, that in your own way you bring to life the evangelical miracle of the multiplying of the bread. To achieve, as you do, on the humble guitar, the sounds, the brilliance, the movement, the variety of tones, the effects of vigour and feeling of a full orchestra, is no less prodigious than feeding thousands of hungry Galileans with four loaves of bread. The Middle Ages would have burnt you as a sorcerer, or venerated you as a saint. Our own age, being less fanatical, is content to marvel at you, as you make it, profoundly impressed, your own.' (1916)

§

In his autobiography, *Morning without Noon: Memoirs*, the Spanish poet, historian, critic, diplomat, and novelist, Salvador de Madariaga, writes about some of his close friends:

11

'Chief among them was the great Andrés Segovia, known to me from the days when he had risen on our horizon in Spain, before he became a musical star of the first magnitude for the whole world. He has achieved perhaps for the guitar what Casals has for the cello, a near-revolution in the way of playing it and of drawing out of it the potential wealth of beauty it had so far concealed; but in at least one way Segovia's achievement was wider and more complex, not merely musical but sociological and psychological as well; for he received from tradition a popular instrument, fallen from the status the *vihuela* had enjoyed in centuries gone by, to conquer the taste and imagination of the people of Spain, who do wonders with it but in a different, so to speak, sociological key; and this instrument it was which by faith, science and will-power, Segovia raised to the sovereign status it enjoys today among the best musicians.'

§

After his debut in Denmark in 1927, *Politiken* in Copenhagen published the following report:

'This young Spaniard is really a phenomenon, just as the rumours said. We have never heard anyone who can possibly be compared with the way he plays his guitar. With his incomprehensible virtuosity and his sense of taste, proving the high level of his musical culture, he makes the guitar an instrument on which proper music can be performed . . .'

§

Manuel de Falla is quoted as saying:

'It is true that with us the idea of "playing on the Spanish guitar" has somehow acquired a curiously disreputable significance, whilst the instrument itself is – or was until the arrival of Andrés Segovia – regarded as a piece of romantic stage furniture.'

§

Ida Haendel wrote:
'Spain had a Velázquez, a Cervantes, a Falla, and there is Andrés Segovia whose genius I have had the privilege to admire through the years.'

§

Yehudi Menuhin wrote:
'In Andrés Segovia there dwells that quiet fire – fierce yet controlled – which is the mark of the Spaniard.
'Where other peoples must rekindle their fires whilst yet others cannot govern them, the supreme artistry of a Segovia, of Casals, of Conchita Supervia, of Victoria de los Angeles, or of Placido Domingo, is proof of an eternal flame – inextinguishable because fed by every great civilisation and race which could cross the Mediterranean – diagonally, lengthwise or crosswise – for thousands of years.'

§

Luciano Pavarotti wrote:
'. . . certainly the Maestro is responsible for bringing classical guitar *"al massimo dello splendore"*. . .'

§

Joaquín Achúcarro wrote:
'Those of us lucky enough to know him personally

13

have had hundreds of occasions to witness the combination of pride and humility which makes a great artist and a great man. One such occasion occurred in 1980 when he greeted me in his hotel suite, his face full of happiness and said, "How wonderful! I have found a new fingering for this passage. So far, it only went well at home. But yesterday, also in concert!"

'(. . . Shall we ever know what "well" means for him?. . .)'

Childhood

'When I was six years old I heard the town band. They were marching along and playing. But I heard not only the tune they were playing, but another in the bass, a countermelody, which I still remember. My uncle then saw my vocation for music.'

§

'. . . all the musicians who were in the little village, instead of attracting me to the instrument, they repelled me. Because they played very badly and it was impossible to suffer the sound of the violin, the cello, the storm of the piano, and so forth.

'Then somebody passed by with a guitar, playing flamenco. I did not like the strumming, the *rasgueados*, but when he did something different, then the guitar captivated me from that moment. I was very attentive to what he was playing, to such an extent that he offered to give me lessons, and then in less than one month, I learned everything that he knew – I mean, very little! At that time I was six years old. Then I had to institute myself as my teacher and my pupil.'

Granada

'. . . I am from Granada, because I spent all my child-
hood in Granada and I opened my eyes to beauty in
Granada. Because when I went in the forest of the
Alhambra I was always in ecstasies.'

§

'The beauty of Granada is quite different from the
beauty of Córdoba. Córdoba is in a kind of plain and
Granada is mountainous. Granada is like a beautiful
woman who looks at herself, and Córdoba – you have
to find that beauty in Córdoba, as well as in Sevilla,
goes suddenly to a corner.'

16

The Spanish

'Spain is a nation of thirty million kings. We have no artistic schools, like the Flemish or the Raphael school of painters, or the classical school of composers. We have only individuals.'

§

'The guitar is an individualist, and that is why she is the favourite instrument of the Spanish people, the most independent in the world. Every Spaniard is a community to himself, just as every guitar has within herself a whole orchestra.'

§

'Allow me to say with pride that the guitar, by being deeply Spanish, is becoming universal. Spain took the guitar because the Spaniard has so rich an individuality that he is a society in himself, and the guitar, by her rich polyphonies and tone colours, is an orchestra in itself.'

17

Moving On

'I launched my real career in Sevilla, where a critic friend wrote that my first show was empty and that in the second show the audience dropped considerably. An artist has to move on.'

Ramírez

The story of how Segovia acquired his first concert guitar, prior to his debut in Madrid at the Ateneo, has been related in various publications; perhaps the most moving account, however, is given on *La Guitarra y Yo* (Decca DL 710182), where Segovia speaks about several incidents in his early career.

On arriving in Madrid, Segovia went to the workshop of Manuel Ramírez (1866–1916), hoping, as pianists were accustomed, to hire an instrument for his big forthcoming recital in the Spanish capital. Ramírez brought out his finest instrument, which Segovia examined for some time and then began to play. After playing some pieces he was spoken to by another visitor to the shop, Don José del Hierro, professor of violin at the Royal Conservatoire of Madrid. Don José warned the young guitarist about the obscurity of the instrument and recommended that he should follow a career as a violinist where there were more prospects, advice which Segovia politely but firmly refused.

Following this encounter, Segovia pressed Ramírez for confirmation that he would indeed hire out this magnificent guitar:

'Ramírez, sensing my eagerness, in a burst of generosity, declared, "The guitar is yours, young man. Take it with you throughout the world, and may your labours make it fruitful. For the rest, don't worry, pay me without money."

'I put my arms out to embrace him, my eyes full of tears. And I said, with a voice so broken that my words could hardly be heard,

"This is one of those acts that have a value, but no price."'

Segovia played the guitar of Manuel Ramírez for the next thirty years, taking it indeed throughout the world.

§

In a travel book about Spain, published in 1922, the authors, Jan and Cora Gordon, tell of their meeting with José Ramírez, brother to Manuel Ramírez, who made Segovia's first guitar of quality. José had instructed his younger brother how to make guitars and, like Manuel, had a great reputation in Madrid. Jan and Cora Gordon were introduced to Ramírez by their Spanish guide, Jesús Pérez, who apparently was a fine amateur guitarist. The authors ordered a guitar from Ramírez, who promised to deliver it in three months at a price of three hundred francs. Ramírez then turned to Pérez and the following conversation took place:

'"And the guitar I made for you," he said, turning to Pérez, "you gave it to S——?"

'"Yes," said Perez.

'"See here," said Ramírez, turning to us, "I make a

guitar, an excellent one, one of my best. This fellow comes to see me, he hears the instrument. He says to me, 'Ramírez, keep that guitar for me, and I will at once go to work in a French munitions factory, and I will work like a slave, and every week I will send you money until the guitar is paid for.' And I agree. And he goes and makes aeroplanes, and does honest work for the first time in his life, I believe, and every week he sends money to me. And the week it is all paid up he stops work and goes off with the guitar. And he is crazy about the instrument. And he goes back to Spain and then he hears S—— playing. He is so enraptured by the wonderful playing of the man, that he runs home, fetches his guitar, and thrusts it into S——'s hands, exclaiming: 'Here is an instrument worthy of you. It is too good for me, for I am a mere bungler beside you.' And so he gives away the guitar that he has laboured for. Ah yes, you villain, I have heard of you."

'As we went down the hill, Pérez tried to explain away this generosity so characteristic of his impulsive nature.

'"It is not as though I would have played on the instrument again after having heard S—— touch it. Every time that I wished to play I would have thought, 'Ah yes, but if only *he* were playing it and not I.' And I had to give it to him, or perhaps I would never have been able to play again."'

Out of discretion Jan and Cora Gordon have not named the mysterious S——, presumably because they were referring to someone well-known. Perhaps it could just possibly have been none other than Andrés Segovia?

§

One evening, when Segovia was playing a recital in Berlin, just before the end of the concert during a quiet *pianissimo* section, there was a loud cracking sound as his guitar split. He went into the dressing room where he repeated sadly to himself, 'My guitar, my guitar' many times.

The cellist, Gregor Piatigorsky, followed him into the room and consoled him.

Later, Segovia found out that the very moment the guitar had cracked had been the moment that Manuel Ramírez, the great guitar maker of Madrid, had died.

Four Tasks

'I always say that I have in life four tasks: the first to redeem the guitar from the folklore; second, to go to every part of the civilised world to show that the guitar is worthwhile to be on the concert stage; the third to create a very good repertoire for it; and the fourth, to influence the authorities of conservatories and musical academies and universities to teach the guitar properly.'

On First Recording

'I made my first recording in Havana, and I was moved, do you know, to the bones, because I heard myself for the first time. When I was ten years old, I always thought it was a great pity for me that I was going to die without listening to my playing. But eventually, I could listen.'

Arbós

There was a celebrated Spanish conductor and violinist, Enrique Fernández Arbós, influential in arranging concerts, but for some reason he disliked the guitar and refused to organise any concert whatever for Segovia, who was a young man in Madrid at the time.

Arbós enjoyed a reputation as a great raconteur and wit, and was, naturally, immensely popular at various parties and soirées where Segovia was also present. But Segovia, disappointed and annoyed by Arbós' lack of enthusiasm for the guitar, did not find the jokes particularly funny and looked singularly unamused when Arbós began telling his stories. Arbós was disconcerted by the young guitarist's rather frosty reception of his anecdotes, but still did not arrange any recitals for Segovia. But at one such occasion, Arbós told a story so hilarious that even Segovia's reserve was overcome and he was convulsed with uncontrollable laughter; the following week Arbós told him that he had managed to arrange some recitals for him.

On Clairvoyance

At a particularly troubled time in his life, Segovia's family thought things might be helped if he sought the advice of a famous clairvoyant who lived in the neighbourhood and who was renowned for her prophetic wisdom and uncanny insight. Segovia was reluctant to go, but after the family had exerted some pressure and discussed the matter thoroughly, he was finally persuaded to give it a try.

He walked through the courtyard and up the stairs to where the clairvoyant had her apartment. He knocked loudly on the door, but nobody appeared. He knocked even louder, drumming on the door. At last, after several minutes, a woman's voice from inside the apartment called out,

'Yes? Who is it?'

Segovia decided that her clairvoyance didn't amount to much, and left immediately before she could open the door, vowing never to seek such advice again.

A Private Recital

When Segovia first played in the United States in 1928 he discovered, to his annoyance, that he was booked to play a recital in a private house, something he did not approve of.

After arriving at the house in Proctor, Vermont, where he was staying, he put on his dress clothes and came downstairs ready to be taken to the recital. He then discovered that he was actually playing at the very house where he was staying. There were three people in the audience, his elderly hostess, her companion, and her brother.

The hostess had attended Segovia's Paris debut in 1924, and had therefore booked him for a recital at the normal concert fee.

Segovia found it was very enjoyable playing for them.

The First Time in an Aeroplane

'It was in 1931, from Mexico to Columbia. In a DC3, which was one of the best planes that Douglas had made. (I have flown many times in South America and Europe in this type of plane.) At first there were thirteen people inside, then fifteen, and then I think, a few more. And there was no possibility of landing as the airport was not prepared. We had to scare the cattle away before we could land. The trip from Buenos Aires to Miami lasted five days, because to fly during the night was impossible.'

Encounter

One day, driving towards Paris, Segovia was overtaken by a particularly bad driver, who seemed to have little control of his vehicle and cut in rather too close at far too high a speed. Some miles later, Segovia saw the same car by the side of the road, apparently broken down. He drew up alongside to give the offending driver a piece of his mind for the previous bad driving. Winding down the window on the passenger's side, he was about to speak when he recognised the driver of the other vehicle.

'Hello, Pablo. What's the problem?'

'This car is no good; it's broken down. Can you give me a lift to Paris? I'll leave this wreck here.'

'Certainly. Hop in.'

So Pablo Picasso left his car by the roadside and accompanied Segovia to Paris.

On Nervousness Before a Concert

'The guitar is very curious. I always say the guitar behaves unpredictably because of the influence of its feminine curves. When I go to a concert I am always nervous; then when I have to begin the concert, I am ready to cancel it; but when I have finished the concert, I would like to begin again.'

§

'We have to conceal our nervosity. We have to contain the animal within. The Prince of Aragon was a great soldier, a great captain, and when he had to go into battle he began to tremble. Addressing his own body, he used to say, "You are trembling . . . well, you will see where I am going to put you now!" and he ran to the front of the battle.'

30

Jazz

In 1933, when Andrés Segovia was in Paris, Michel Prunières, an official of the Hot Club (whose father, Henri, edited the *La Revue Musicale*) organised a reception at his father's house. The purpose was to introduce the great jazz guitarist, Django Reinhardt, to Segovia. Django arrived with his brother, and played a few pieces, but Segovia remained distinctly unimpressed.

§

'I once heard a man play jazz on a guitar. He had only two fingers on one hand and he did it very well. But it was not what I would call music.'

The Visitor

During World War II guitar strings were very scarce and precious. After a concert in Montevideo, at a time when Segovia was short of sets of strings, a man visited the Maestro in the artists' room. He opened a bag to reveal several sets of excellent strings.

'Wonderful,' said Segovia. 'How much do you want for them? I would like to buy them.'

The man replied that he didn't want to sell them, he was just showing Segovia how many sets of strings he possessed.

The Beggar

After completing part of his regular morning practice sessions, Segovia used to take a brisk walk, sometimes buying a newspaper at the kiosk near his home in Madrid. During this constitutional, Segovia would frequently pass by the favourite haunt of one of the district's most well-known beggars, a blind man with a great reputation for his self-possession, dignity, and occasional caustic wit. (In Spain, unlike the customs of north European countries, the beggars regard themselves as followers of an honourable and ancient profession, whose existence is spiritually beneficial to those Christian souls who dispense charity – preferably on a regular basis – whether large or small, to such unfortunates.) Segovia's footsteps had long been known to the beggar and the Maestro was in the habit of giving a few *pesetas* on each occasion and passing the time of day as he did so.

However, one morning, preoccupied with a new composition that had been offered to him, Segovia found himself without convenient change in his pocket and on his return towards home was compelled to walk past the beggar without having anything to give him.

'Forgive me, señor,' said the Maestro, 'but I have no *pesetas* with me this morning.'

'Well, in that case,' replied the man, 'if that's how things are, you can find yourself another beggar to give your money to.'

J. S. Bach

'Together we would run through the *Well-Tempered Clavier* and a few of the beautiful Bach choral works. His greatness overwhelmed us.'

§

'Bach was like a gigantic tree of which an Andalusian, graceful master of exaggeration, used to say, "If it is tall, it takes two men to look at it; when one gets tired, the other comes and begins to look where the other left off until he reaches the top." Between my friend and me, we were able to perceive the majestic grandeur of the master.'

§

'The best public are those who understand the character of the music I play and everybody's reaction is the same. Because a person who is sensitive to Bach reacts the same if he belongs to the south, the north, east or west.'

'I am a guitarist but I also love Bach. So I play him on my guitar so that I can show the expressive side of his music, the noble, the serious and the dignified. And, also, the beautiful.'

The Guitar

'The guitar shouldn't be too loud; one harmonic can be heard throughout the Festival Hall. It's the clarity of the guitar that carries, not the volume.'

§

'I can make my guitar sound in any concert hall, provided I have a co-operative audience.'

§

'The guitar must proceed this,' [his hands shape a series of parallel vertical lines], 'but the player, in his mind, must think like this' [a single undulating horizontal line]. 'The fingers must work free of the mind. The sound of the guitar is very small, much smaller than a harpsichord. Therefore, the listener must be at a distance and when he is at that distance, he no longer hears the vertical lines separate from each other. He hears the horizontal line. We must always watch inspiration from afar. Do not come too close, or the poetry disappears.'

'The sound of the guitar is not voluminous, but luminous.'

§

'. . . sonority and its infinite shadings are not the result of stubborn willpower, but spring from the innate excellence of the spirit.'

§

'Of all the solo instruments, the guitar is the best. It has poetry, unlike the harp or the harpsichord. The harp is wonderful in an orchestra, but as a solo instrument the ear soon begins to tire. And I told Wanda Landowska that the harpsichord sounds like an instrument that has caught a cold – it is very nasal. But the guitar contains all the colours of the orchestra.'

§

'I deliberately chose the guitar because it was an instrument that belonged to the people. Its traditions are steeped in folklore. It is very poetic.'

§

'The guitar is a total experience. It is a world of music in one small frame. It is the instrument that describes the soul of Spain.'

§

'The guitar is the purest and most total instrument. You play just one simple phrase (not a symphony or a concerto) and it satisfies.'

'The guitar is best without the orchestra; that is why I no longer play concertos. The guitar imitates all the colours of the orchestra – the violins, the oboe, the cellos, the brass – but when the guitar plays *with* the orchestra, all these colours are already there, so the guitar sounds tiny and that is all.'

§

'The guitar is like a tiny orchestra, seen through the wrong end of a pair of binoculars. It is polyphonic and contains many different timbres. It has all the colours of an orchestra. It can sound like a flute or an oboe or like strings.'

§

'I would like everyone to listen to the lovely natural voice of the guitar. A guitar should be shaped simply and with a feminine quality, like an honest woman. It should be built to produce many voices, many colours.'

§

'You know that the guitar has feminine curves and this influences her behaviour. Sometimes it is impossible to deal with her, but most of the time she is very sweet; and if you caress her properly, she will sing beautifully.'

§

'When the guitar is played with love and skill, there issues from its melancholy sound a rapture that holds us fast to it forever.'

'I have dedicated my life to two things – to my wife who is my living guitar, and to my guitar who is my singing wife. And concerning the sacrifice, I think the real sacrifice for an artist who loves music is to be apart from his instrument and not to dedicate *all* his work and leisure to his instrument and music.'

§

'The guitar was trapped in a vicious circle: it was not studied in the conservatoires with the result that there were no guitarists; there were no guitarists, so no composers wrote for the guitar; there was no music, so no one took up the guitar. A vicious circle.'

§

'The guitar of the early nineteenth century was small. Also, they only played in small concert halls; and many of them played with the little finger on the body of the guitar. Imagine, always playing in the same place! Freedom of the hand is essential for the orchestration, the colouring.'

§

'When did you learn to play the guitar?'
'Before my birth, I think!'

§

'A humorist once said to me, "The piano is a rectangular monster whose teeth you scrape to make it howl, and stringed instruments only make a noise when you flog them. The guitar alone responds to persuasion."'

'Listening to the persuasive voice of the guitar, I said to myself, "How is it possible that such a beautiful instrument has no serious music composed for it?" My friends came to my rescue by helping me to find the kind of music that I was looking for.'

§

'From my youthful years I dreamed of raising the guitar from the sad artistic level in which it lay. At first my ideas were vague and imprecise, but as I grew in years and my love for it became intense and vehement, my will to do so became more assertive and my intentions clearer.'

§

'There is a legend more beautiful than the true historic facts. It pretends that Apollo once upon a time was running to catch a wonderful nymph, and when he succeeded in taking her into his arms, she invoked her semi-divine father, who instantly changed her into a beautiful tree – the laurel. Apollo made the guitar out of this tree, by reason of which the curves of the guitar allude to its feminine parentage. And not only the curves, but the spirit too, is highly feminine. For the guitar is the most unpredictable and least reliable musical instrument in existence – and also the sweetest, the warmest, the most delicate, whose melancholic voice awakens in our soul exquisite reveries.'

§

'My life's ambitions are fulfilled. A whole new generation of classical guitarists has been born to carry on my work, and they will have their hands full. The classical guitar is just beginning.'

41

Interpretation

'My artistic ideals are to achieve union with the work I am interpreting – giving all to it in such a way that it owes something to me. I love the story of the widow's son of Nain, although it has no proper ending. So I found a conclusion for it. Christ stops the funeral cortège, raises the young man and delivers him to his mother, saying gently, "He is alive: take back your son." Then the mother says to Jesus, "Lord, don't you think that he belongs to you a bit too? It's true I brought him into the world but haven't you brought him back to life?" I think the conversation of the interpreter and the creator is like that.'

§

'But as for us pianists, violinists, cellists and guitarists – how many hours of pain and self-abnegation, how many weeks, months and years do we spend polishing a single passage, burnishing it and bringing out its sparkle? And when we consider it "done to a turn", we spend the rest of our life persevering so that our fingers shall not forget the lesson or get entangled again in a brambly thicket of arpeggios, scales, trills, chords, accents and grace notes! And if we climb from that region of technique to the more spiritual sphere of interpretation, what anguish we experience in trying to find the soul of a composition behind the inert notation, and how many scruples and repentings we have before we dare to discover what does *not* lie hidden in the paper!'

§

Andrés Segovia and the great pianist, Ignaz Friedman, a renowned Chopin specialist, were very good friends and once, by coincidence, were both undertaking tours of South America. Thus they found themselves together in Buenos Aires, and each having a few days to spare, decided to attend a piano recital by Artur Rubinstein. They obtained seats in the front of the circle to the right of the platform. Rubinstein, on raising his eyes during an especially soulful passage, seemed visibly astonished at the sight of the two musicians sitting there. Either for that reason, or through the excessive heat of the summer evening, the pianist did not perhaps achieve his best form, making a particularly poor showing in the works of Albéniz and Chopin (the former, of course, being one of Segovia's own favourite Spanish composers).

After the concert, Segovia and Friedman went backstage to tender their respects to Rubinstein. Friedman approached Rubinstein first and, smiling sweetly, remarked, 'How I enjoyed your playing of Albéniz.'

Segovia, in his turn, also smiled graciously, and murmured, 'And how I enjoyed your Chopin.'

On Being Self-Taught

'I became my own teacher – and also my own pupil. It is still so, only now the teacher is more nearly satisfied.'

§

'I have been my teacher and my pupil, and both have got along very nicely without serious quarrel.'

§

'The man who is given by heaven the vocation of music, knows how to struggle with everything provided to become a musician. This was my case.'

Guitar Students

'There are two million guitar students in Japan alone.'

§

'My disciples – many of whom are already famous teachers and artists – will continue my work, fervently adding their own artistic contributions to the history of this most beautiful instrument.'

§

In an interview published in the *Tacoma News Tribune*, Segovia gave his reason for not wishing to give a talk before a student gathering. He said:

'An artist should remain a mystery. He should just play.'

Freedom and Discipline

'If you look at a tree, the roots are fixed on the land, on the earth, and nevertheless the higher part of the tree moves with the wind. That means it is necessary to have a great discipline and to fix this discipline, and then to move with the emotion of the moment.'

Technique

'Out of difficult passages I made a new exercise. Often I ceased to regard the motif I had chosen as part of a specific work, and elevated it to a superior level of studies in which was latent the promise of victory over more general difficulties.'

§

'The practice of scales enables one to solve a greater number of technical problems in a shorter time than the study of any other exercise.'

§

'Build a technique to cover all the difficulties of the piece, slowly with efficiency. Play pieces on your own level or below and gradually you arrive at your goal. The angels of Jacob came up and down the ladder step by step, although they had wings.'

47

'Most of the pupils here in class are trying to play pieces much beyond their capacity. They are not prepared, musically or technically. There are many beautiful compositions on the same level as your technique. The students who are not well advanced and are playing the difficult pieces are committing a sin against the music, the composer, the guitar, and the people listening.'

§

'If I interrupt you, it is because I think it will be better for you.'

Practising

'You can never have sorrow for more than two hours a day when you practise. It brings happiness.'

§

'We guitarists – or any serious musicians – need the stern discipline of life-long practice, many years of self-denial. Many hours and weeks polishing a single passage, burnishing it to bring out its true sparkle. The creation of beautiful imagery demands the cares of gestation and the pains of childbirth.'

§

'I am very fond of practising, you know, because always I find something that should be changed. Normally, I practise one hour and a quarter in the morning, then I rest. I take a deep bath, etc., I shave, and then another hour and a quarter. And then in the afternoon I will resume without fatigue; because with fatigue it is absolutely impossible to practise well –

49

whether mental fatigue or muscle fatigue – with any sort of fatigue it is impossible. A friend of mine used to answer when accused "You work very little time", "Yes, but my hours are cubic hours!"'

Paris

'When I first came to Paris, Joaquín Nin introduced
me to Henri Prunières, the editor of *La Revue Musicale*,
and very important in the musical world. All the great
artists played in his concerts, which were held in a hall
on the ground floor at street level. However, I noticed
that every sound of traffic could be heard. When the
monster of the piano is playing, or the violin, or the
cello, it is all right, but not for the guitar. So when
Henri Prunières asked me would I like to play, I said
"No".

' "No?"'

'This was unheard of, no one refused.

'But when he offered that I should play at his own
home, then I accepted.

'He gave me two big scores to use as a footstool. One
was Rossini. I didn't like to do this to Rossini, to put
my foot on him.'

§

'The first concert I heard in Paris was the pianist
Alfred Cortot. Later, I met him and we became good

51

friends. We called each other "godfather" and "godson". When he wrote to me he always addressed me as "My dear godson".'

§

'In Paris, a high-up military man, who also composed, wrote something for me. However, he believed that I was courting his girl; but this was a thing which I never did to my friends.

'I was playing a concert there and some mutual friends asked him,

'"Are you going to hear Andrés tonight?"

' "No! No! No! I never would!"

' "But why not?"

' "Because if I am in the audience and he knows that I am there, he will play even better!" '

§

'The social background to a musician's life in Paris was not always easy. Wanda Landowska and Respighi were invited to the residence of the Princesse de Polignac. But the butler took them to a different room – musicians were not to be with the guests.

'Later, a telegram arrived at the hotel where I was staying with Respighi, inviting him again to the Princesse de Polignac's.

'"Not possible," he answered, "I am here with my friend, the guitarist Andrés Segovia."

'Another telegram arrived: "I invite you, Mr Segovia, and all your friends."

'This time, *I* replied: "We would be happy to be your guests, but please ask your butler first if we may come in!"'

Manuel de Falla

When Segovia was accompanying Manuel de Falla on a trip to Venice, they found they could never make an early start because Falla was busy taking many kinds of medicine to ward off imaginary illnesses. Segovia said to him,

'Manuel, why such zeal for medicines? They will think in heaven you haven't Faith that they will protect you.'

Falla went scarlet and walked out. It seemed like the end of the trip, but eventually he returned and said earnestly,

'Swear not to repeat this in my lifetime. Swear! But I am not like the donkey that carries the Holy Relics to which everybody kneels, and then believes the homage is for itself. I am in receipt of a gift from God, but I don't want to bother Him with the care of my body, which is of no importance.'

Thus, with nobility and dignity, Falla carried on taking his precious medicine all the way to Venice.

§

Jaime Pahissa, Manuel de Falla's biographer, tells of the journey Segovia and Falla made together in 1932:

'After San Sebastián, Falla had to go to Venice in response to an invitation to conduct *The Puppet Show* at the International Festival of Music. Knowing this, Andrés Segovia, who wanted a short rest after a strenuous series of concerts, sent Falla a telegram suggesting that they should travel together from Geneva, where he was then staying. He proposed that they should make the journey by car, stopping at interesting places on their way. Falla gladly accepted, but asked whether he could also bring a friend, Dr José Segura, a professor from Granada University. They took the train to Geneva and left for Venice in Segovia's car. They went by way of the Simplon, saw the North Italian lakes, drove through Milan and stopped in such wonderful Italian cities as Verona, Vicenza and Padua before arriving at Venice.

'In Venice several problems concerning the arrangements for the concert arose, and Andrés Segovia said that he solved them by diplomacy. The programme consisted of *The Puppet Show*, a work by Lualdi and *Maria Egiziaca*, by Respighi. Falla was not very pleased to find that his work was to figure in a programme beside a piece with such a plot as that of *Maria Egiziaca*, in which Respighi describes the licentious life led by the Saint before she gave herself up to mortification and penance.

'Yet another difficulty arose over the order of the programme. When they arrived in Venice they found that this was to be, first *The Puppet Show*, then *Maria Egiziaca* and finally Lualdi's work. Segovia rightly thought that it was disrespectful to Falla to have his work as the opening item of the concert and, although Falla, with innate modesty, would have accepted this, Segovia would not allow it and had the programme

54

altered so that it began with Lualdi's work followed by *The Puppet Show*, with *Maria Egiziaca* last.

'Here *The Puppet Show* met with its greatest success . . .

'They returned in Segovia's car. Falla had a very unpleasant boil on his right temple, which he attributed to an infection contracted from having shaken hands with so many people who came to congratulate him and which he had transferred to his forehead when putting on his glasses. In fact, the condition affected his whole face and threatened to become very serious. On reaching San Remo, they had to stop to find a doctor. They were dressed in dusty travelling clothes, Segovia with long, unkempt hair, Falla with his face distorted by the swelling and pain. His friend Dr Segura was at least dressed with a tidiness which contrasted with the disorder of his companions. They went into the doctor's house, and Segovia introduced Falla with suitable eulogies as "the great composer, Manuel de Falla", and Falla likewise introduced the great guitarist with similar praise. The doctor regarded them distrustfully, as though he feared they were lunatics. Then they introduced Dr Segura, who presented a more correct appearance. "Here's a more likely-looking person," exclaimed the doctor, shaking hands with him. The upshot was that he treated Falla very successfully, so that by the same afternoon they were able to continue their journey to Arles.'

§

Segovia himself disputes the accuracy of the last story as told by Pahissa. What actually happened was that Falla, being rather nervous by disposition, disliked seeing any doctor except his own personal physician, but events made immediate medical attention very

55

necessary. Falla steadfastly refused to consult any doctor, but the boil was swelling and growing and extremely painful.

Segovia secretly contacted a doctor and arranged for him to meet Falla, bringing with him, surreptitiously, his little medicine bag. He was introduced to Falla as a music-lover, and while they were talking together, the doctor removed a scalpel from his bag without letting Falla see it. While he was saying how much he admired Falla's music, the doctor suddenly leaned forward and lanced the boil, piercing like a picador!

After this, the problem was, more or less, solved.

§

'Falla had a wonderful story to set to music, of a Saint, Maria, who lived on an island. So as to get to church to pray, she gave her body to the oarsman who rowed her across to the mainland where the church was.

'Respighi heard the plot and used it himself for an opera.

'In Venice, Respighi was very excited and keen to meet Falla, and kept asking me to introduce him. But Falla, on hearing how Respighi had used the plot, had threatened violence, so I kept them apart. Until Respighi cottoned on and asked why I was avoiding the meeting; then I told him the truth finally, and things were all right after that.'

Segovia's career has progressed from listening reverently to being listened to reverently by the greatest: (*left*) Segovia, seated second from left, listens to the playing of Miguel Llobet; (*below*) details of the concert Segovia gave at the White House in 1979 *Courtesy of the Carter White House Photo Office*

President and Mrs. Carter
Honor
Andrès Segovia

A Concert
at
The White House

Sunday, March 11, 1979

Program

Song of the Emperor and 'Diferencias' on a Spanish Tune *	L. de Narvaez (Ca. 1538)
Fugue (Originally for Lute) *	J. S. Bach (1685-1750)
Theme and Variations Menuet in A	F. Sor (1778-1839)
Melancolia (Dolce e Mesto) Primavera (Quasi Toccata)	M. Castelnuovo-Tedesco (1895-1968)
Allegretto Castellano	F. Moreno Torroba (Born 1891)
Sevilla *	I. Albeniz (1860-1909)

*Revised and adapted by Andrès Segovia

CENTRO ARTÍSTICO

DE

GRANADA

SEXTO Y ÚLTIMO CONCIERTO

POR LOS EMINENTES ARTISTAS

ANDRÉS SEGOVIA

(GUITARRA)

Gaspar Cassadó y Gabriel Abreu

(VIOLONCELLO Y PIANO)

EN EL TEATRO DEL ALHAMBRA-PALACE-HOTEL

EL DIA 2 DE MAYO DE 1918

CASA SABATEL, Gran Via, 12 - GRANADA

Real Academia de Santa Cecilia

DE CÁDIZ

CONCIERTO

POR EL

EMINENTE GUITARRISTA

Don Andrés Segovia,

PARA EL MARTES 19 DE MAYO DE 1914

— PROGRAMA —

PRIMERA PARTE

Gavota en *la* menor.....	*Tárrega.*
Estudio en *la* n.º 24	*Coste.*
Capricho árabe.........	*Tárrega.*

SEGUNDA PARTE

Bourrée.........	*Bach.*
Sonata, op. 13, adagio...	*Beethoven.*
Nocturno	*Chopin.*

TERCERA PARTE

Granada, serenata.......	
Cádiz, saeta	*Albeniz.*
Sevilla	

Á LAS NUEVE Y MEDIA DE LA NOCHE

Early concert announcements

Drawing by Miguel del Pino y Sarda for a recital by Segovia in Madrid in 1920

Segovia in the 1940s, from the record sleeve 'Andrés Segovia'
Courtesy EMI

Segovia in the 1970s *Courtesy Ibbs & Tillett Ltd*

Segovia in his studio in Madrid *Graham Wade*

In England, with his guitar and silver-topped cane – at Wakefield Station in 1983

Courtesy Yorkshire Post Newspapers Ltd

At the Westbury Hotel in London, 1985: (*above*) with his son Andrés and daughter-in-law Antje and (*below*) with Graham Wade

Segovia on tour in Scotland: in his dressing room at the Village Theatre, East Kilbride in 1984 *Photo by A. Watson, courtesy East Kilbride News*

At the Barbican in London in 1984 with him is Stewart Warkow, who has just handed over the famous silver-topped cane prior to the interval.

On stage in 1985

On Writing for the Guitar

'I do not commission new works, but once they hear how their music can sound on the guitar, composers are eager to write for it.'

Manuel Ponce

Manuel Ponce of Mexico, with Segovia's help, played a Kreisler/Pugnani-like joke on the musical public. Ponce composed some pastiches of Bach, and it was intended to play these pieces in recital. However, mindful that Wanda Landowska, and scholars like her, might attend a concert by Segovia, it was decided that it would be unwise to pass off these works as being by the great Johann Sebastian himself. Ponce and Segovia, therefore, selected the name of the great lutenist Sylvius Leopold Weiss, the friend of Bach whose actual compositions were less well-known at that time than they are today. Other works by Ponce were attributed to Alessandro Scarlatti.

In the case of the 'Weiss' pieces, it was not long before several editions of these works appeared in print, allegedly researched from original manuscripts, but undoubtedly taken down from Segovia's recordings.

A *Gavotte* by 'Alessandro Scarlatti' was played by John Williams in 1958 on his first recording; the sleeve-notes mentioned that the piece was 'discovered by Andrés Segovia in a manuscript in Naples Conservatoire . . . harmonically they contain more than a trace of "modernity",' perhaps implying that the writer of the notes was in the know.

On a Segovia recording of the 1950s containing some of these pieces, the sleeve-notes comment: 'These three movements are from a *Suite for Lute* by a little-known (undeservedly so) contemporary of J. S. Bach, Sylvius Leopold Weiss . . . Though the manuscripts of this lutenist are rare, those surviving reveal a happy combination of masterful counterpoint and beguiling melody.'

Eventually, in the late 1960s, the secret was revealed, though as late as 1974 one writer of sleeve-notes described these pieces as 'from Weiss' *Suite in A minor* arranged by Ponce'.

One result of Segovia's performance of these pastiches in many recitals throughout the world, was a growing interest in the works of Weiss, who was ultimately established as a prolific and worthwhile composer of the high Baroque.

Flamenco

'My first audience in Granada could not conceive that the Spanish guitar was for anything but flamenco. I have spent a lifetime trying to redeem the guitar from flamenco.'

§

'Now flamenco – by which I mean popular song, dance and guitar-playing which has become folk-lore. I think the professionals have destroyed the charm, the spontaneous charm of flamenco.'

§

'I love flamenco, but the *true* flamenco – not the flamenco heard these days. The flamenco guitarist of today has removed his attention from the ideals of yesterday when this noble art was prized for a depth of emotion which could be produced by a certain simplicity of approach. Today's guitarists are more theatrical, they want to show their technique, to dazzle the public with pyrotechnics. And so they not only insert chords not belonging to the true flamenco, but they also

60

emphasise the rapid scale passages, tremolos, and so forth. The result is not to my taste.'

§

'Manolo de Huelva played in a *very* simple manner, very flamenco, just as it should be, being folklore. He never resorted to a cheap display of pyrotechnics; his playing was simple, emotional and expressive . . . Yes, Manolo de Huelva was the best during the time of my youth.'

§

'We have never before had such a magnificent assortment of flamenco guitarists. They are marvellous, every one of them. The problem is that none of them plays flamenco. How can you expect them to play flamenco? Who understands flamenco? This art is felt and understood by a tiny group of Andalusians – not even by the average Spaniard, mind you – and foreign audiences certainly have no idea what flamenco means.'

§

'There was a flamenco guitarist among a group of singers and dancers. The audience asked him to play alone. So he left the singers and dancers and played on his own.

' "No!" they shouted. "On your own!"

'The guitarist came to the front of the stage and played again.

'And again they shouted, "No! Alone!"

'"What do you mean?" he called to them.

'"When we have gone," they answered. "Alone, on your own!"'

61

Critics

Diego Rivera, the greatest of modern Mexican painters, was asked by Vasconcelos, the Minister of Education, to decorate the patio of the ministry with frescoes.

One day, Andrés Segovia arrived at the building and was somewhat startled to see the painter standing on the scaffold, brush in hand, wearing a holster and two large revolvers.

'Why those two pistols at your girdle?' asked Segovia.

Rivera, with his bitter-sweet Mexican accent replied,

'As a guidance for critics.'

§

In an interview with Segovia, Bernard Gavoty asked:

'Do you remember that curious engraving we noticed one day at the Cabinet des Estampes? It showed David, as king, holding three musical instruments – a lute, a kind of theorbo and a psaltery – with an immense two-edged sword to unify the whole composition. Now why the sword?'

62

According to what had been worked out before the interview, Segovia should have replied, 'Because David was not only a conqueror but also a devotee of music. For this reason he could both overcome the Philistines and enchant Saul.'

However, somewhat mischievously, Segovia responded, 'Perhaps David had seen a music critic peeping over the horizon . . . which proves that David was not a very good musician, because a true artist is no more scared of critics than an honest man of the police.'

§

'I was playing Castelnuovo-Tedesco's *Sonata Omaggio a Boccherini* in Turin. The local critic gave the work a terrible review and said it reminded him of a French popular song. It was such a bad review I didn't send it to Castelnuovo-Tedesco. But he, Castelnuovo, received all reviews from an agency, so he read it all the same. He immediately wrote a set of variations on that French popular tune, finishing up with a magnificent fugue. I sent it to the critic, who later admitted that he had been unjust.'

On Coughing at Concerts

'Well, what I did in Madrid (and other places), was a very amusing thing. They were coughing just as I was playing a piece by Bach which was very delicate and very slow. I stopped playing and I looked up. Then I took my handkerchief and I put it like that [coughing gently]; of course, when you put the handkerchief in your mouth like that you have no noise, no disagreeable noise, and if you cough that way it is perfectly all right.'

§

'It's quite easy to stifle a cough if you work at it.'

§

In noise ratings for audiences, Segovia estimated that Britain and America are perfect for playing, Scandinavia and Germany are fine, but in Italy and Spain, though the cities are good, the suburbs are not so good.

64

Literature

'I like philosophy, history and poetry; and best of all
the poetry of – can you guess? – not Lorca, but
Antonio Machado, the greatest poet of our time. I
knew Lorca, though. He was captivating, charming.
He lived one year in New York without learning
English – he was *waterproofed* against the language.
  'I can read from Spanish, English, French or
Italian, but I cannot read many authors of today with
their dirty words and without punctuation. Even the
good authors do that.'

§

'When I am not practising I work on my autobiography. I write with a pencil in order to erase. I think I
erase more than I write.'

Food

'Food? Keep it simple. No sauces or gravies. I eat
steaks and chickens, always grilled.'

§

Whilst enjoying a particularly sumptuous dinner,
Segovia remarked to his guests, 'The silence compli-
ments the food.' He then went on to tell a story of a
dinner party where talking was not allowed, the main
concern being the excellent quality of the food. However, one guest, invited to such a dinner, constantly
made appreciative noises: 'Mmmmm, mmmmm.' The
host said afterwards, 'We won't invite him again – he
talks too much.'

On Languages

'When I speak in English I can only express half of what I think, and the listener can only understand half of what I say.'

§

'I speak French like a native of Paris, English with difficulty, and German only in self-defence.'

Three Kisses

'I was asked if I would play for the writer, Benito Pérez Galdós, at his home, and of course I was delighted. He had illuminated my life with his many writings, but now he was old and blind.

'I knew he loved Beethoven so I played for him Tárrega's transcription, arranged by myself, of the slow movement of Beethoven's *Pathétique Sonata*. As I played, a filament of sound accompanied the melody. He sang all the way through, softly.

'At the end, he took my hand and kissed it.'

§

'When I first visited Russia in 1926, the custom, when kissing a lady's hand, was to bow down low to the hand. As I did this, the lady kissed me on the forehead.'

§

'Pizzetti was there, and d'Annunzio's son, and Toscanini. After I had played, Toscanini kissed my hand,

and dedicated a score to me. This score, along with six thousand books and manuscripts, was lost when I had to leave my home in Barcelona when the Civil War broke out.'

On Politicians

'Once there were three friends. The first said, "My profession is the oldest in the world – I am a surgeon. When the Lord made woman she was made from one rib of man. This is a surgical operation, thus my profession is the oldest."

'The second said this: "My profession is older than yours. Before man and woman were created, God had to separate the light from the darkness. That is the work of an engineer. I am an engineer. Mine is the oldest profession."

'The third said: "Not at all; before the Lord made the universe, there was chaos, and I am a politician."'

§

'All artists are democrats, except Liszt and Paderewski, who liked to float among the aristocracy.'

In Hospital

In 1953, in a private ward of a hospital in Madrid, Segovia, nearly sixty years of age, played the guitar for a few close friends. He had just undergone an operation for a detached retina and his sight was threatened. He wished to find out if he could still play, even if he was blind. To prove he could, he played the *Fugue in A minor* by J. S. Bach, after which he announced, 'Good. Now I am ready.' However, Dr B. Carreras, a Spanish eye specialist, was so skilful that after a month spent in bed without moving his head, Segovia regained his sight. He still had over thirty years of recitals throughout the world to give.

Masterclass

A Mexican guitarist had been roundly rebuked by Segovia during a masterclass at Siena. The Maestro, in some exasperation, had remarked, 'Your thumb makes a terrible sound on the strings. Why don't you do something about it? Cut it off if you have to – perhaps you'll grow another one.'

The recipient of this advice was understandably depressed and began to drink heavily. A friend asked him what the matter was, and the guitarist replied that he was waiting for the tower to open at three o'clock, when he would climb to the top and throw himself down, because of the bad tone of his thumb.

Segovia was told about the Mexican's state of mind, and rapidly approached the man as he was leaving the café and walking towards the church with the high tower.

'Don't do it, young man,' said Segovia. 'If you cut the thumb off, the new one might sound even worse.'

Modernism

'Abstract painting and concrete music! Both are denials of true art!'

§

'I am too old to accept this terribly dissonant music. The composers are experimenting now with noise. When the noise will be sound and the sound will be music, I will have an opinion.'

§

'While the tuning of the guitar continues to be the same, it is an instrument for consonant music. That doesn't mean that delicious dissonance cannot be played, but there are many composers today that have used that. But not the cacophony. In a piece by a French composer, whose name I do not wish to mention, a Sonata for piano is played with the fist. But with the guitar, that is impossible. It is so delicate an instrument, so poetic, that it is impossible.'

73

'Modern music, like modern painting, is now often strident, discordant. One of our Spanish artists painted a large circle with a blue dot in the centre – what talent! And that was Miró!

'Sometimes modern composers put instructions on the score of their music for the player to "improvise as you wish" for several bars – we could all write that kind of music!'

On Music

'Music is like an ocean and the instruments like small islands. Some are flat, others mountainous, some are florid. The guitar is one of the most beautiful of the islands. I say that as a musician and not as a guitarist.'

Pop Music

'I have heard of these Beatles, but what they play is strange to me. I do not think it is anything to do with art as I know it. I do not like the movements of the boys, the loud electric guitars, the cries, the way the girls go crazy. I distrust quick popularity. An artist should concentrate on his guitar with all his life, and let his public come later. We guitarists – or any serious musicians – need the stern discipline of life-long practice, many years of self-denial.'

§

'I like to steal the young people away from their heroes.'

§

When George Harrison of the Beatles acclaimed Segovia as 'the daddy of us all', Segovia remarked: 'The Beatles are very nice young men, no doubt, but their music is horrible. Even as illegitimate children I could not accept them.'

§

'I do not like it. What is this noise they make? What does it mean? It means nothing. It is plebeian.'

Amplification

'It alters the beautiful sound of the guitar, nullifies it, renders it acid and metallic. From a loudspeaker you can still appreciate the artistry of the performer, the agility of his fingers, but you do not have the true sound of the instrument. I tell my students not to use amplification.'

On Facial Expressions

'I hate all the artists who make faces or gestures while playing or conducting. Music is more serious than that. Many young conductors whose real academy is the mirror, do violent movements with the arm, with the body, with the face, and that is absolutely insincere. That belongs more to an actor than to a musician.'

Jerez

In Jerez, in Andalusia, they have made a sherry barrel
in honour of Segovia. Other recipients of this honour
include Napoleon.

Noise

In 1967, Segovia was booked to play at the City Hall, Newcastle. The organisers forgot, however, that the swimming baths were next door. The *Northern Echo* reported that 'whistle blowing, duck-boards banging, doors slamming, young swimmers yelling, frequently drowned Segovia's softer passages for many of his listeners', and made the suggestion that Newcastle City Council should end this discourtesy to both artists and concert-goers, either by curtailing evening swimming sessions or by adequately sound-proofing the dividing walls. Segovia's comments on the occasion have not been recorded.

Los Olivos

Segovia wanted to have a house built at Almuñéca, on the southern coast of Spain. While on a concert tour in New York, the architects brought him the choice of three plans of the house. Segovia chose one of the designs, which looked well-proportioned and worthwhile. However, he forgot to look at the scale of the house, and when the house was built he got a shock at the size of it. It included a thousand square metres under cover, as well as extensive gardens, and needed a resident staff to look after it when Segovia wasn't there.

His Son, Carlos

Segovia's youngest son, Carlos, was asked at school, along with all the other children, what his father did for a living. Some of the others had already disclosed that their fathers were engineers or doctors. Carlos carefully explained that *his* father was a guitar student.

§

'The other day in school, he was the only boy in the class who could answer a question. The teacher went over to him and pencilled a moustache on his face over his lips.
    ' "Carlos," she said, "You're a man now."
'That gives me a lot of pleasure.'

§

'He is very proud of being born in England, in St Mary's Hospital, Paddington. When he is asked if he is a Roman Catholic, he always says: No, he is an Anglo-Catholic, and a Liverpool supporter.'

Linares

In the town where Segovia was born, Linares, in the province of Jaén in northern Andalusia, Spain, they have dispensed with the usual chimes of the Town Hall clock in the main *plaza*. Instead, on the hour, the clock plays a few snatches of *Estudio sin Luz* (Study without Light), one of the Maestro's best-loved compositions.

Also in Linares, a distinguished citizen has bought a special apartment in which is housed a comprehensive collection of Segoviana, including discarded bowties, full medical records going back many years, all his recordings, thousands of recital programmes and their subsequent reviews.

Visitors going to see this Segovia collection, have on occasion been surprised to see their own letters to the Maestro, carefully collected and preserved among the treasures of the Museum.

Travel

'I lead a sedentary life at five hundred miles an hour.'

§

When Segovia travels by air, he always goes first class. He books two seats in the front row of the plane, always on the left side, one seat being for the guitar. He also carries with him his famous silver-headed cane.

§

'Travelling is part of my keep-young policy. Music helps too. Also hard work. But most important of all is to keep moving. I am on the move from one part of the world to another the whole time.'

§

'Like the poet, I can say: "I have felt the roundness of the world beneath my feet."'

85

Wives and Guitars

'I've had three wives and three guitars, though I have flirted with others.'

On Fatherhood

'I have become better known as a father than for my art.'

Heaven

There is a story that an enthusiastic but very old and frail admirer of Segovia went to a recital by the Maestro. Overcome by excitement and heat, the poor man fainted and was taken off to hospital, where regrettably he later expired.

In the afterlife, the man hurried towards the Gates of Heaven; approaching the Pearly Gates he heard the sound of guitar playing not unlike that which he had heard on earth. At the Portals of Heaven stood St Peter, to whom the departed soul addressed himself:

'Excuse me, sir, but I thought I heard guitar playing. Is Segovia here?'

'Not at all; Segovia is well and on earth. But you are certainly here.'

'But that guitar playing is wonderful . . . Who is it, please?'

And St Peter answered,

'That is God, trying to play like Segovia.'

Segovia's Prayer

'Do you know my prayer? I will say it. "My Lord, I am a great sinner. I do not deserve the glory of being in Heaven with You, so, if You are agreeable, let me remain here." For the time being, He is listening to me.'

Recitals

At seventy-nine years old, in 1972, Segovia was still giving fifty to seventy-five concerts a year in Europe and the United States. According to *Reader's Digest*, his estimated income from this was £100,000 annually. Most of his thirty long-playing records have sold over a million copies, and at that time, brought in a further £40,000 a year.

§

In 1985, at the age of ninety-two, Segovia gave half a dozen recitals in the United States, several recitals in Germany, five recitals in England, and five in Italy.

§

At the age of eighty, Segovia said:
'This year I've restricted my engagements to thirty-two; eighteen in Europe and fourteen in the United States. In October I toured the Continent, then returned to Madrid for a rest. From January until March I'll be playing in the United States.'

On Philosophy

'Life is too big and too large to be enclosed in a principle. First, to live, and then the rest. *Primus vivere, deinde philosophare.*'

Old Age

'I am absorbed in youth. Do you know, the tragedy of the old man is that he continues to stay young in all ways, but the people around him don't see it.'

§

'You will see in my audiences more and more young people. It is from them that I draw my youth.'

§

'I am already becoming something from the past.'

Final Word

'Enough. I pride myself only in having been a daring tireless prober of the subtle beauty of the guitar . . .'

Conversations

(Segovia talks to Graham Wade in Madrid, 1983)

W. Have you practised today, Maestro?

S. Oh yes, already very early. I sleep very little in the
night and waken at five o'clock in the morning,
even if I go to bed at two o'clock. But as I am
restless and do not want to disturb my wife, I
come up here to my studio and practise for one
hour and a half.

Then I shave and have my breakfast, and then I
do the same – practise another hour and a half.
And so, without effort, I have already practised
nearly three hours, and no fatigue. You cannot
practise beyond fatigue; it is absolutely no use.
You cannot keep the attention fixed so long on
what you are doing. I do not believe the artists
who say they practise eight hours a day – they are
a liar or an ass! You may work the whole day and
the whole night, but it is a deception. It is different, of course, when you are given a new work
which awakens your enthusiasm and your interest; then you *could* work the whole day and the
whole night! But this is exceptional.

95

W. How do you proportion the practice time?

S. Half an hour daily to exercise the fingers and to make them flexible. Then, if you have a concert, you play these pieces for the rest of the time.

W. Do you still play scales and slur exercises?

S. Yes, but not excessively, because it is not so much necessary when the fingers are already active and flexible. Unless, of course, you had to spend two or three days away from the guitar without any playing.

W. I would like to ask about the composers who have written music for you.

S. The first composer who answered positively to my request was Federico Moreno Torroba. First he composed the *Danza* which is in the little *Suite Castellana*. After that he composed much much more, because when once a composer has heard a composition of his on the guitar, he will never stop composing ˙for the instrument, never. Mario Castelnuovo-Tedesco, Heitor Villa-Lobos, and Joaquín Turina were certainly the same. The only composer who wrote only one piece, but is worthy of many, was of course Falla.

W. When composers wrote for you, did you have to change the music somewhat?

S. Always I have to modify many things. But we do this so as not to betray the music and so that we do not omit what the music has to offer, but in order to make the music better for the instrument. I am accustomed, you know, with the composers who have written for me, to modify something or other in almost every bar.

   For instance, with Castelnuovo-Tedesco, he always had a mania for including a march in every piece. A march! Until I said, 'Please, no march!' I don't know why he was so fond of marches. I remember I laughed with him about it. He was a fine composer.

Even with Villa-Lobos I had to modify. I told him that the last section of his *Etude No.7* was not idiomatic for the instrument. I wanted it to be changed or I could not play it. The trills there do not sound idiomatic for the guitar. Anyway, I went to the recital (I was playing in Paris at the time), and he sent me a telegram in which he said, 'All right – play it the way you wish – I like it very much.'

W. How would you compare the music of Castelnuovo-Tedesco with that other prolific composer for the guitar, Manuel Ponce?

S. Castelnuovo-Tedesco writes beautifully always, but like this [waving his hand in a straight horizontal line]. Ponce writes like this [waving his hand downwards to indicate depth and profundity]. Ponce is the greatest for the guitar, melodically, harmonically and musically. You know, in Ponce everything is magnificent for the guitar, melody, poetry, everything, even the Concerto. The Concertos of Castelnuovo-Tedesco are very beautiful, but the Concerto of Ponce is better. The harmony is so beautiful, and not the conventional harmony out of a text-book Method of Harmony.

W. And what about Joaquín Turina – you knew him well?

S. Turina? Oh yes, he was a very very good friend. But Turina had no idea how to write for the guitar. *Sevillana* was the first piece he wrote for me. I had to keep sending it back and every three days he wrote it all out again. Everything he wrote included the theme of the *Sevillana*. When he came to write *Fandanguillo*, he wanted to put the same thing in again, and I had to say no! And of course,

Fandanguillo is a most beautiful composition. But with the *Sevillana* I had to work very hard; I had to make many modifications so that it could be more fluent over the fingerboard. And he was a perfectionist himself in every way. And every day came another version if there was anything I disliked. And one day, he gave me a *whole* sonata.

W. But you didn't play the *Sonata* by Turina very much, did you?

S. I played the *Sonata* on one tour and no more. That was because the themes are not really those of a sonata at all. Look at the sonatas of Ponce – all the themes are appropriate to the form of a sonata [sings themes from Ponce, then from Turina]. Turina's themes are like a very robust lady doing the movements of a dance, they are not defined.

W. And Turina's *Homage to Tárrega*, I can't remember that you ever played that one either? But it's popular with a lot of recitalists.

S. No, I do not like it. The *Homage to Tárrega* has nothing whatever to do with Tárrega. It has a *Garrotín* and a *Soleares,* and is very Andalusian. Tárrega was from a little place in Valencia, from Villarreal, and lived in Burriana.

W. And *Ráfaga* – you didn't do that one!

S. No, not that either. The *Sevillana* and *Fandanguillo* are the pieces that remain throughout my career.

W. And was Turina *simpático* as a person?

S. ¡*Oh sí, sí, sí*!

§

S. What have you been doing this morning?

W. We went to see some publishers quite near here. It was in the street called Cochabamba.

98

S. Cochabamba! That street is named after a town in South America. I have been there. It's in Bolivia at a height of some three thousand metres. I played a concert there and also at La Paz.

W. Was it a good place to visit?

S. Well, when I first arrived, I went to stay with an important person of the town as a guest in his house. But what a room he put me in – I went over to the bed, pulled back the cover, and the sheets were dirty, absolutely dirty. I went to the leader of the Spanish delegation there and said, 'When does the plane leave for Buenos Aires?' He said, 'Well, you could get one later in the week.' And I replied, 'I mean *today!* I want to go *now!*'

W. It sounds like a good place to leave! But what about the altitude? Doesn't that make things rather difficult?

S. Oh yes, it takes quite a while to become accustomed to the thin air. After a day or two, because of the altitude, I felt breathless, so I asked the Spanish Ambassador to send a doctor. But the usual doctor was away, it seems, so they sent an Indian doctor. He said to me, 'Flex your legs twenty times,' and showed me the way I had to do it. I commented, 'I am more inclined to "*re-flexion*" than flexing!' but all the same I flexed my legs and even did a couple extra flexings, making it twenty-two times. When I had finished, the Indian doctor said, 'There is obviously nothing wrong with your heart, because if there had been, you would be dead after all that exercise.'

W. Cochabamba sounds rather a dangerous place to be!

S. As a matter of fact, several members of the Spanish delegation died there. One took a cold shower after a hot bath, and collapsed. Another died in

99

the bathroom after getting out of the tub. And the third was more joyous – he was drunk most of the time anyway.

W. Well, what with giving recitals there, you were lucky to survive the experience!

S. As soon as I got back to Spain I went to the physician for a full medical examination. He told me my heart was so good I could have gone to the Himalayas!

But there is one consolation – when the inhabitants of Bolivia come down to sea-level, they *also* have a problem. When I was in La Paz, the Mayor took me to a bullfight. There were four toreros, whom I recognised. However, the bulls were brought from Peru, so when the bulls entered the ring, the four toreros stood well back, and by the time the bulls had crossed the ring and reached the toreros, the animals were short of breath and puffing badly.

W. Did they have picadors in the bullring there?

S. Yes, but they didn't have much to do!

§

W. Do you have many guitars, Maestro?

S. Not at all. Some American friends of mine are collectors of collections! But I do not do this, and have only four or five guitars in my house. My entire house would be populated by guitars if I kept all the guitars which people wish to send me. But I return them with kind words encouraging them to continue their good work.

W. Apart from the first good guitar by Manuel Ramírez, what other fine instruments do you recall?

100

S. The first good guitar was by Ramírez, the great uncle of the modern founder of the Ramírez company. The second was a Hauser. I have also played guitars by Fleta, but now I also play Ramírez, the later ones.

W. But the Hauser was one of the best?

S. I think the best. And sometimes, because of the son, the tradition can be carried on. But now, you know, the Hauser guitar has been sleeping for a very long time.

W. What about your original great Ramírez?

S. One day, I have the idea of giving the Ramírez of 1913 to the Conservatory of Geneva, which was the first place to create a post for the teaching of the guitar. But I could not teach there myself because I was obliged instead to give my concerts. But later, after the war, I suggested a suitable professor for them to appoint. But it is still very difficult to find suitable professors for the conservatories. Too many people think that only playing concerts is worthwhile. It is important to learn how to teach well. Sometimes, I ask at Siena, or Santiago de Compostela, or the Metropolitan, New York, or Geneva, or other academies and universities where I have given classes, 'Who is your teacher?' Because often it is terrible and students have been very badly taught.

W. A lot of people praise the old Torres guitars.

S. Well, no, no. Torres had to make a living by making guitars for the people who played popular music and flamenco, people who had no interest in the quality of sound. Also, they were quite small instruments. Then he made a good guitar for Arcas and another for Tárrega; but that was not enough. And then, I think his guitars did not have sufficient volume.

101

Do you know, a rich American went to Llobet and said that he would give one *duro* (five pesetas) for each ornament on the rosette of a Torres guitar to anyone who could find the best Torres guitar for him. Of course, after that, a huge quantity of Torres guitars appeared everywhere!

Then, whenever I was giving a concert in Spain, there was always someone who brought a guitar to me. They were all looking for a Stradivarius of the guitar. But the guitars they brought me were always unsuitable. And so I said, No, no, no, and I always played, during the first part of my career, the guitar that was made in Madrid by Ramírez. If there had been one suitable, I am sure I would have seen it sooner or later.

W. What about the problems of modern guitar making compared with the early years of the twentieth century?

S. Nowadays, perhaps because of the wood, it is very, very difficult. The guitars do not always seem to have the same quality. Then, as well, some of the higher notes, above the twelfth fret, do not have the good sonorities that are necessary. The sound of the notes is often very uneven.

W. Apart from the problems of making guitars, there are many problems nowadays travelling with guitars, what with jet travel, central heating, and different climates.

S. Oh yes. I have three or four guitars of Ramírez and two Fleta guitars. The Fletas are very nice, the sound is very good. But I made the mistake of taking one of the Fletas to the United States in winter. I went to the hotel room, turned off the heating, and opened the window for five minutes in order to cool the atmosphere. But the man in the room upstairs, and the man in the room downstairs, and the man in the room next door, hadn't done the same, so the walls held the full force of the blazing heat. One month later the guitar cracked, and I had to telephone my wife to send out another guitar – a Ramírez, the Ramírez guitars are stronger. The problem is that the Americans heat the rooms as though it is summer, even when it is winter. In all the shops, everyone is in shirt-sleeves because of the heating, yet outside it is bitterly cold.

Dates in Segovia's Career

1893   Born in Linares, province of Jaén, Andalusia, Spain, 21 February.

1904   Moved with his family to Granada.

1909   Debut at the Centro Artístico, Granada.

1911/12 Recitals in Córdoba, Sevilla, Cádiz, Huelva, Granada. Heard piano recital by Alfred Cortot in Córdoba, 'my first religious experience in music'.

1913   First recital in Madrid, at the Ateneo.

1917   Extensive tour of Spain.

1918   Further recitals in Spain; married for the first time.

1919   First foreign tour; departed from Cádiz for Uruguay and Argentina. His son, Andrés, born in Argentina.

1920   After a return to Spain, further recitals in South America.

1922	Played recitals at Manuel de Falla's *Concurso de Cante Jondo* in Granada.
1923	Recitals in Cuba and Mexico. First meeting with Manuel Ponce. First meeting with Heitor Villa-Lobos. 17 December, premiered Turina's *Sevillana* in Madrid.
1924	Debut in Paris, 7 April.
1924/5	Recitals in Switzerland, Germany, Austria.
1925	Première of *Segovia*, *op. 29* by Albert Roussel. Turina's *Fandanguillo*, *Op. 36* composed, completed 4 June.
1926	Recitals in Russia, 2 March, and Britain, 7 December. First publication 'Guitar Archives–Edition Andrés Segovia' (B. Schott's Söhne, Mainz).
1927	Recital in Denmark, 29 April. First recordings for HMV.
1928	Recitals in United States. Some transcriptions for guitar of music by J. S. Bach first published.
1929	First meeting with Joaquín Rodrigo. *Douze Études* by Heitor Villa-Lobos composed. Recitals in Japan.
1931	First trip by air.
1932	First meeting with Mario Castelnuovo-Tedesco. Trip to Venice with Manuel de Falla.
1935	First performance of transcription of Bach's Chaconne, in Paris, 4 June.

1936	Leaves Spain following outbreak of Spanish Civil War.
	Married for the second time.
1939	Première of Castelnuovo-Tedesco's *Concerto in D, Op. 99,* in Montevideo.
1941	Première of Manuel Ponce's *Concierto del Sur,* in Montevideo, October.
1947	First post-war appearance in London after an absence of nine years.
1949	Made his first long-playing record, 22 and 30 June.
1956	Première of Heitor Villa-Lobos' *Concerto for Guitar and Orchestra,* Houston.
1958	Première of Joaquín Rodrigo's *Fantasía para un Gentilhombre,* San Francisco, 5 March. Founding of Summer School at Santiago de Compostela.
1961	First recital tour of Australia.
1962	Married Emilia Corral Sancho.
1967	The film, 'Segovia and Los Olivos' made. Awarded Gold Medal for Meritorious Work (Spain).
1970	His son, Carlos Andrés, born in London.
1974	Received Degree of Doctor of Music, *honoris causa,* Oxford University.
1976	Autobiography published in the United States.
1977	Recorded *Reveries* album, 20–24 June.
1978	Became member of the Spanish Royal Academy of Fine Arts.

1980   *The HMV Recordings, 1927–39* issued by EMI on long playing records.

1981   Awarded the title of Marquis of Salobreña by His Majesty, King Juan Carlos I of Spain.
The Albert Schweitzer Award.
Segovia International Guitar Competition, Leeds Castle, Kent, England, 9–13 October.

1982   Recital tour of Japan.
Masterclasses in the Metropolitan Museum of Art, New York.

1983   His ninetieth birthday celebrated by a recital tour of the United States.
Awarded Degree of Doctor, *honoris causa,* Cádiz University.

1985   Recitals in the United States, Britain and Italy.
Awarded Gold Medal for distinguished services to music by the Royal Philharmonic Society.
Statue of Andrés Segovia unveiled in Linares, May.

Acknowledgements

The author would like to express his appreciation to all those who have contributed in any way towards the compilation of this book. In particular, my profoundest gratitude is due to Maestro Andrés Segovia and Señor Alberto López Poveda.

Grateful acknowledgement is made to the following sources by reference to page number and (in brackets) the number of the item on that page:

Morning without Noon: Memoirs, by Salvador de Madariaga (Saxon House, Farnborough, 1974), page 11(2), 62(1).
Manuel de Falla and Spanish Music, by J. B. Trend (Alfred A. Knopf, New York, 1929), 12(3).
Segovia – A Celebration of the Man and his Music, by Graham Wade (Allison & Busby, London, 1983), 13(1, 2, 3 & 4).
BBC Woman's Hour, 15(1 & 2), 30(1), 35(3), 64(1).
BBC Celebration Interview with Michael Jessett, 16(1 & 2), 30(2), 44(2), 46, 79, 91.
BBC Christmas Interview 1978, 24, 28, 44(3), 49(3), 73(3).
Segovia on Stage, Alan Rich interview on sleeve notes for

recording MACS 1032, 17(1), 36, 37(3).

Florida State University, Tallahassee, Andrés Segovia's acceptance speech on receiving the degree of Doctor of Music, *honoris causa*, 27 February, 1969, 17(2), 41(3).

Chicago Sun-Times, 23 March, 1983, 18, 39(2), 75, 92(3).

La Guitarra y Yo, Decca DL 710182, 1971, 19 & 20, 35(2), 47(1).

Poor Folk in Spain, by Jan and Cora Gordon (John Lane, The Bodley Head Ltd., London, 1922), 20 & 21.

Cellist, by Gregor Piatigorsky (Garden City, New Jersey, 1965), 22.

Music and Musicians, 1973, 23, 37(2), 41(4), 90(3).

Reader's Digest, October, 1973, 27, 44(1), 76(2), 85(1), 90(1).

The Observer, 2 October, 1977, 31(2), 38(5). 10 May, 1970, 38(6), 60(1), 26 March, 1978, 49(1).

Django Reinhardt, by Charles Delaunay, trans. Michael James (Cassell, London, 1961/Ashley Mark Publishing Co., Gateshead, 1981), 31(1).

Segovia, An Autobiography of the Years 1893–1920, by Andrés Segovia (Macmillan, New York, 1976/Marion Boyars, London, 1977), 35(1), 41(1), 93.

Diatonic Major and Minor Scales, by Andrés Segovia (Columbia Music Co., Washington D.C., 1953), 38(2), 47(2).

Radio Times, 1977, 38(4), 64(2 & 3), 66(1), 83(2), 85(3), 86, 92(1).

Daily Express, 1967, 39(3), 49(2), 76(1).

The Guitar and I, sleeve notes on record MCA 3965, by Andrés Segovia, 39(5), 85(4).

Andrés Segovia, by Bernard Gavoty (René Kister, Geneva, 1955), 40(4 & 5), 42(1 & 2), 62 & 63.

International Herald Tribune, 20 March, 1980, 38(1), 39(4), 57, 78.

Sunday Telegraph, October, 1981, 45(1), 65(1 & 2), 83(3), 89.

Tacoma News Tribune, quoted in *Guitar News*, 45(3).

Guitar News, from a masterclass at the North Carolina School of Fine Arts, 1966, 47(3): from a conversation with Segovia by Samuel Chotzinoff, 1962, 73(1).

Guardian, 29 October, 1979, 53, 70(2), 82.

110

Manuel de Falla, His Life and Works, by Jaime Pahissa (Museum Press Ltd., London, 1954), 54 & 55.

John Williams Guitar Recital, sleeve notes on record Delysé ECB 3151, by John W. Duarte, 1959, 58 & 59.

An Andrés Segovia Recital, sleeve notes on record Brunswick AXTL 1005, *c*. 1955, 59.

Guitar Review, No. 42, New York, 1977, 60(2), 61(2 & 3).
    No. 52, New York, 1983, told by Oscar Ghiglia, 72.

Daily Mirror, 1967, 71, 77(2), 92(2).

Northern Echo, 1967, 81.

Acknowledgement is made to the following for permission to reproduce photographs:

East Kilbride News (Photo by A. Watson), for the photograph of Segovia in the artists room; The Carter White House Photo Office, for the photograph of Segovia playing at the White House; EMI, for an early portrait; Ibbs & Tillett, for a concert portrait; Yorkshire Post Newspapers Ltd., for the photograph of Segovia arriving at Wakefield Station.

I would also like to thank the following for supplying interesting information and sources of various kinds over the years:

Wilfrid M. Appleby, Peter Beaver, Vladimir Bobri, Els Breukers, Arnie Brown, John W. Duarte, Gabriel Estarellas, John Mills, Cobie Smit, Maurice J. Summerfield, Bengt Wikström, and Gerta Zelt. I am also indebted to my wife, Elizabeth, for research and help in the preparation of the manuscript.

Several of the anecdotes and sayings can be found in various sources; if, however, any owners of copyright material have been inadvertently omitted, I would like to express my grateful thanks to them.

111